For Jill Bennett
with every happy wish,
Eve Merriam

Books by Eve Merriam

A Word or Two with You

New Rhymes for Young Readers

A Word or Two with You

New Rhymes
for Young Readers

BY EVE MERRIAM

ILLUSTRATED BY JOHN NEZ

Atheneum   New York   1981

LIBRARY OF CONGRESS CATALOGING IN PUBLICATION DATA

Merriam, Eve
   A word or two with you.

   SUMMARY: Original poems primarily about words but
incidentally about friendship, parents, new neighbors, the
supermarket, and other life experiences.
   1. Children's poetry, American. [1. American poetry]
I. Nez, John A.   II. Title.
PS3525.E639W6   811'.54   81–1282
ISBN 0–689–30862–0   AACR2

Text copyright © 1981 by Eve Merriam
Illustrations copyright © 1981 by Atheneum Publishers, Inc.
All rights reserved
Published simultaneously in Canada by
McClelland & Stewart, Ltd.
Manufactured by
American Book–Stratford Press, Inc.,
Saddle Brook, New Jersey
Designed by M. M. Ahern
First Edition

For Waldo and Jonah

Contents

Secret Hand

I closed my eyes
and made a fist of my hand:

I held a stripe
from the tiger tree,
an emerald snowflake,
a drop of orange rain,
and thirteen purple
grains of sand.

Then
I opened my fingers
and I let them
fly free.

Tube Time

I turned on the TV
and what did I see?

I saw a can of cat food talking,
a tube of toothpaste walking.

       Peanuts, popcorn,
       cotton flannel.
       Jump up, jump up,
       switch the channel.

I turned to Station B
and what did I see?

I saw a shampoo bottle crying,
a pile of laundry flying.

       Peanuts, popcorn,
       cotton flannel.
       Jump up, jump up,
       switch the channel.

I turned to station D
and what did I see?

I saw two spray cans warring,
a cup of coffee snoring.

       Peanuts, popcorn,
       cotton flannel.
       Jump up, jump up,
       switch the channel.

I turned to station E
and what did I see?

I saw dancing fingers dialing,
an upset stomach smiling.

       Peanuts, popcorn,
       cotton flannelette:
       jump up, jump up,
       turn off the set.

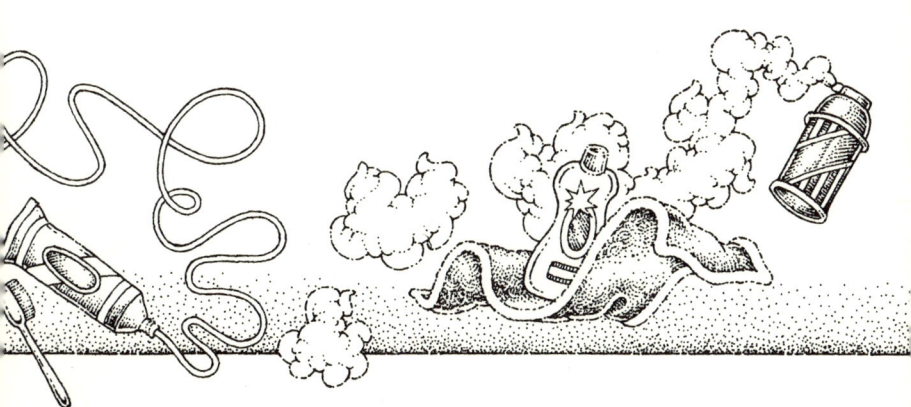

Out of the City

"Eugene,"
said Claire,
"let's drive somewhere
and picnic in the open air."

"Keen,"
said Eugene,
"the air will be clean,
and the grass will be green."

So they drove
and they drove
and they drove and they drove
and they drove and they drove
and they drove
                    and they drove
until they found
some open ground
where they hurried and ate
because it was late
and then turned the car around

and they drove
and they drove
and they drove
and they drove

and they drove
and they drove
and they drove
and they drove
back from the clean green scene.

The Dreadful Drawkcab

It's live and evil,
it will step on pets,
set part of a trap,
stab at bats,
turn a star
into rats.

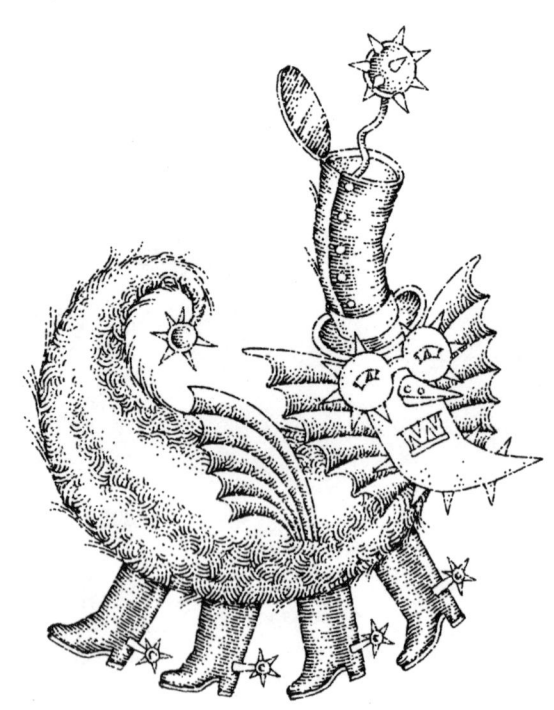

Supermarket, Supermarket

(A JUMP ROPE RHYME)

Supermarket, supermarket,
shelves piled high
with brand-new products
for you to buy:

Vegetable soapflakes,
filtertip milk,
frozen chicken wings ready to fly,

shreddable edible paper towels,
banana detergent,
deodorant pie.

Shh

If I covered up my ears
I couldn't hear
car horns honk
garbage cans clang
screen doors bang
toasters tick
or crickets crick

or telephones ring
or foghorns hoot
or grease spatter
or fire crackle
and sigh to ash

or paper crumble
or thunder crash
or the squeak of a rocker
or the shout of a crowd
or the crack of a nut
or a motorboat's putt.

But
could I hear a feather
or a snowflake
or a cloud?

What Is a Rhyme?

A rhyme is a chime
that rings in time.
Ding, dong,
come along.

One word herding with another,
like a sister and a brother.

Do you know Sue and Lou,
Millie and Billy,
Pearl and Earl,
Vicky and Ricky,
Sal and Al
and Jess and Tess?
Yes?

A rhyme is like two feet
down the street:
run, rhyme, run!
Chase the sun!

A rhyme can be short:
Hi, Guy!
'Lo, Joe.

A rhyme can be long
if you serve Thanksgiving turkey
to a family in Albuquerque,
or you have a hippopotamus
that makes a lot of fuss.

A rhyme can chime at the *end* and also in the *middle:*
Come on, be my *friend*—tell me a *riddle!*
What's red at the *top* and blue (blew) all *over?*
The wind in a *crop* of sweet rosy *clover!*

A rhyme can be tricky
if you watch a butterfly
flutter by
or turn a handstand
on a bandstand.

What else can you do with a rhyme?

You can take a rhyme and shake it
and wake it up:
come on, rhyme!
time to chime!
   Ding, dong,
   bong!

You can rhyme with two
out of the zoo:
a hare and a bear,
a cow and a sow,
a moose and a goose,
a cat and a rat
and how about a wombat?

With a rhyme you can send
Ned
to bed
(that sleepy redhead)

Make Terry
hurry

Get Don
to put his pajamas on

Sail with Dan
to Japan
along with Stan and Ann

Send Alice to a palace

Have Carrie
marry
Larry or Barry
(or perhaps she'd rather Harry).

Give Jenny
a pretty penny

Put Boris
in the chorus
while Susannah
plays piano
with Knute
on the flute
and Lynn
on the violin
and Grace
on the bass.

What else can you do with a rhyme?

You can shape it and drape it
into a cape
for a lady ape
who is peeling a grape.

You can trounce it and bounce it:
allee, allee in free,
last one in is a donkey!

Want to catch a rhyme, latch a rhyme, attach a rhyme?

Then snip it, trip it, clip it, flip it, tip it, dip it,
and zip it in.

You can store a rhyme with rocks and blocks and hollyhocks
in a box with locks down at the docks.

Pour a rhyme till it passes
like molasses
into glasses
oh
so
slow . . .

Throw a rhyme like a ball
against a tall wall.
                        Fling,
                        zing!

Or launch it like a rocket into outer space
until it fades away with no earthly trace.
Whizz,
here it is
and then when you let go
you can almost hear it echo. . . .
No longer here
but out there
                    somewhere.

Goodbye for now, rhyme.
Meet you another chime-time.

Tell Me a Story

Tell me a story
of eons ago
when the world was not
the world we know:

when dinosaurs roamed
and reptiles flew
and four-footed mammals
upright grew.

Now tell me a story
of women and men
living on the moon—
and what happens then.

A Word or Two with You

The sound of *must*
reeks of indoors
shut up with homework and chores

whereas
volunteer
packs up camping gear
and mountain views
that say Wishyouwerehere.

I Scream

Nicodemus Nicholas Belvedere Brown
is the very best ice cream eater in town.
A cone or a cup,
he'll guzzle it up;
a sundae with sprinkles
gives him the twinkles.
Strawberry, banana, vanilla macaroon,
he can eat ice cream from here to the moon.
He dreams of chocolate chip, dish after dish,
and pistachio's his favorite flavorful wish.
He can't get enough
of the meltaway lipadrip lap-and-lick stuff.
Rocky road marshmallow! Orange mandarin!
Ginger peachy! Pack it all in!

"No," says his mother, "just one portion."
"Well then," says Nick, "may I pick the dish?"
"I guess," says his mother, "I guess you may."
Says Nick, "Hooray."
"Then the dish that I pick is rather small,
Just about the size of a red bouncing ball
that expands to be as big as a bed,
a bed that's so high and so wide and so deep
that inside it ten fat men can sleep
and a horse and a sheep can fit into it too,
along with a dolphin and a kangaroo,
and ten tall ships and ten more again,

and a forest and a farm and a factory and a mill,
and an airplane hangar and the highest hill. . . .

"Stop!" says his mother.
"As soon," says Nicky, "as I fill the dish."
"And that will be all?" his mother says,
"just that one dish that is round as a ball?"
"Of course," says Nick, "for I don't want a portion
that's too big, I wouldn't like to be a pig."

Fiddle-Faddle

Riddle me no,
riddle me yes,
what is the secret
of sweet success?

Said the razor, "Be keen."
"String along," said the bean.
"Push," said the door.
"Be polished," said the floor.
Said the piano, "Stand upright and grand."
"Be on the watch," said the second hand.

"Cool," said the ice cube.
"Bright," said the TV tube.
"Bounce back," said the yo-yo.
"Be well bred," said the dough.
"Plug," said the stopper.
"Shine," said copper.

"Be game," said the quail.
"Make your point," said the nail.
"Have patience," said the M.D.
"Look spruce," said the tree.
"Press on," said the stamp.
"Shed some light," said the lamp.
        "Oh, just have a good head,"
        the cabbage said.

It isn't

It isn't a bud
that turns into a rose,
but it grows.

It isn't a set
of musical bells,
but it yells.

It isn't a hippo
with triple chins,
but it grins.

It isn't a goat
eating paper bags,
but it na-aa-ags.

It isn't a vine
wrapped 'round a tree,
but it trails after me.

It's no other
than
my baby brother.

Portmanteaux

Two separate words
sometimes condense
into a sound
that's more intense:
pairings like those
are *portmanteaux*.

Thus smoke and fog
roll in as *smog*,
breakfast and lunch
are served for *brunch*;
scatter and hurry blur into *scurry*,
rush and hustle run into *rustle*,
chuckle and snort cavort as *chortle*:
so language like
a giraffe's neck grows.

A turtle that's short
may turn to *tortle*,
a grape and a berry be a *grerry*,
a nest in a nut tree form a *nustle*:

so coin new words
and spend and lend
as syllables wander, waft and wend
and blend and bend and never end.

Two People

She reads the paper,
while he turns on TV;
she likes the mountains,
he craves the sea.

He'd rather drive,
she'll take the plane;
he waits for sunshine,
she walks in the rain.

He gulps down cold drinks,
she sips at hot;
he asks, "Why go?"
She asks, "Why not?"

In just about everything
they disagree,
but they love one another
and they both love me.

Frying Pan in the Moving Van

A new family's coming to live next door to me.
I looked in the moving van to see what I could see.
> *What did you see?*
> *Tell, tell, tell.*

Well,
I saw a frying pan in the moving van.
> *What else did you see?*
> *Tell, tell, tell.*

Well,
I saw a rocking chair and a stuffed teddy bear
and a frying pan in the moving van.
> *What else did you see?*
> *Tell, tell, tell.*

Well,
I saw a rug for the floor and a boat with an oar
and a rocking chair and a stuffed teddy bear
and a frying pan in the moving van.
> *What else did you see?*
> *Tell, tell, tell.*

Well, I saw a leather boot and a basket of fruit
and a rug for the floor and a boat with an oar
and a rocking chair and a stuffed teddy bear
and a frying pan in the moving van.
> *What else did you see?*
> *Tell, tell, tell.*

Well, I saw a TV set and a Ping-Pong net
and a leather boot and a basket of fruit
and a rug for the floor and a boat with an oar
and a rocking chair and a stuffed teddy bear
and a frying pan in the moving van.
What else did you see?
Tell, tell, tell.

Well, I saw a steamer trunk and a double-decker bunk
and a TV set and a Ping-Pong net
and a leather boot and a basket of fruit
and a rug for the floor and a boat with an oar
and a rocking chair and a stuffed teddy bear
and a frying pan in the moving van.
What else did you see?
Tell, tell, tell.

Well, I saw a lamp with a shade and a jug of lemonade
and a steamer trunk and a double-decker bunk
and a TV set and a Ping-Pong net
and a leather boot and a basket of fruit
and a rug for the floor and a boat with an oar
and a rocking chair and a stuffed teddy bear
and a frying pan in the moving van.
What else did you see?
Tell, tell, tell.

Well, since you asked it:
I saw a wicker basket
and a violin and a rolling pin and a vegetable bin
and a lamp with a shade and a jug of lemonade
   and a garden spade
and a steamer trunk and a double-decker bunk
   and a Chinese model junk
and a TV set and a Ping-Pong net
   and a framed silhouette
and a leather boot and a basket of fruit
   and a baseball suit
and a rug for the floor and a boat with an oar
   and a knob for a door
and a rocking chair and a stuffed teddy bear
   and plastic dinnerware
and an electric fan and a bent tin can
   and a frying pan and
THAT'S ALL I SAW IN THE MOVING VAN.

Secret Talk

I have a friend
and sometimes we meet
and greet each other
without a word.

We walk through a field
and stalk a bird
and chew a blade of
pungent grass.

We let time pass
for a golden hour
while we twirl a flower
of Queen Ann's lace

or find a lion's face
shaped in a cloud
that's drifting, sifting
across the sky.

There's no need to say,
"It's been a fine day"
when we say goodbye:
when we say goodbye
we just wave a hand
and we understand.

In a Word

If you have a charm
no harm
will come to your arm.

Don't spill
a pill
if you're ill.

He wrote on the slate,
"I'm late
because I overate."

When a body blow
hits too low:
OW!